MANUAL FOR DRUMMERS AND BUGLERS

U.S. MARINE CORPS

DEPARTMENT OF THE NAVY
HEADQUARTERS UNITED STATES MARINE CORPS
WASHINGTON, D. C 20380

14 December 1971

FOREWORD

1. <u>Purpose</u>. To promulgate suggestions, instructions and information pertaining to Marine Corps drum and bugle corps and field music service.

2. <u>Information</u>

    a. This Manual has been compiled as a guide to commanding officers and Marine Corps drum and bugle corps personnel in the utilization and function of Marine Corps drum and bugle corps units and buglers serving as the field music of the guard.

    b. This Manual does not amend any directive promulgated by higher authority; if apparent conflict exists the latter shall take precedence.

3. <u>Reserve Applicability</u>. This Manual is applicable to the Marine Corps Reserve.

4. <u>Certification</u>. Reviewed and approved this date.

E. B. WHEELER
Major General, U.S. Marine Corps
Assistant Chief of Staff, G-1

DISTRIBUTION: 7315001   (25)
               3001/6901001, 002/7501001/8145 (2)

Copy to: 7000019   (25)
          7221001   (2)

PCN 100 013324 00

RECORD OF CHANGES

Log completed change action as indicated.

Change Number	Date of Change	Date Received	Date Entered	Signature of Person Entering Change

TABLE OF CONTENTS

Prologue

HISTORY OF THE FIELD MUSIC

DRUMS AND FIFES

From very ancient times music has been used in conjunction with military operations.

The drum was used in the early civilizations of Egypt, Personal and Greece and was introduced into Western Europe and Britain during the Crusades; it was effectively used to "beat the charge" and to regulate the movement of soldiers in the line of march.

The fife, formerly called the Swiss flute because of the prominence it gained when carried by the Swiss troops in the battles of Marignano in 1515, was introduced into England in 1557. It was first used with the drum for martial music in the British Guards regiment in 1747, and subsequently adopted by other English infantry regiments. British troops on duty in America prior to the Revolutionary War introduced the art of drumming and fifing to our Colonial militia. During that war the drum and fife were the only musical instruments used by our military forces.

The first drummers and fifers in the United States Marine Corps were enlisted as members of the First and Second Battalions of American Marines authorized by Congress November 10, 1775. In our early Navy, two drummers and one fifer were generally assigned to each ship's Marine guard.

On July 11, 1798, President John Quincy Adams approved a bill authorizing the Marine Corps to enlist a drum major, a fife major, and 32 drummers and fifers. Some of these musicians were assigned to recruiting duty and aboard frigates during the French naval wars; however, sufficient numbers were retained in Philadelphia under Drum Major William Farr to form a military band. This band was the origin of the famed United States Marine Band, Washington, D. C., the oldest organization of its kind in the country.

For the next century following the Revolutionary War, drummers and fifers played their part in making Marine Corps history. They served with distinction at Tripoli, in the War of 1812, in campaigns against the Indians in Florida, and in the storming of Chapultepec. During the Civil War the stirring music of the fife and drum rose to probably its greatest heights.

BUGLES

The Franco-Prussian War changed the formation of troops in the field from closed to extended lines. The American Army adopted this method of warfare but found difficulty in controlling extended lines by voice; therefore, in 1875, the use of the fife was discontinued and the bugle was adopted to signal commands. On July 1, 1881, the Marine Corps followed suit. This change was strongly opposed by the fifers in the Corps who tried in every way to regain official support to continue playing their fifes. A music school was established at the Marine Barracks, Washington, D.C., to teach the fifers to play the bugle; however, they still protested claiming they had enlisted as fifers not as buglers. Finally, the colonel in command directed that no fifer would be permitted to reenlist without signing an agreement that he would learn to play the bugle.

In 1892 the Navy issued instructions standardizing all bugle calls. Prior to this the captain of each naval vessel prescribed the calls used aboard his ship which the Marine drummers and fifers were required to know. For example, "Annie Laurie" might be played for morning colors and "Auld Lang Syne" for retreat. Officers evening mess was signaled on some battleships by the playing of "The Roast Beef of Old England." (This has become a tradition in the Marine Corps at formal dinners known as "Mess Nights.") Except for a few minor changes, the bugle calls in use today by Armed Forces buglers are the same as the original calls prescribed in 1892.

THE FIELD MUSIC SCHOOL

In late 1916 the first Field Music School known as the Drum and Trumpet School, was established at the Marine Barracks, Port Royal, South Carolina (now the Marine Corps Recruit Depot, Parris Island). Between April 6, 1917 and November 11, 1918 the school graduated 493 field musics. The school has remained in operation continually since its inception and now trains all field musics and drum and bugle corps personnel in the Marine Corps.

In 1934 the need for more competent drummers and buglers was recognized by Headquarters Marine Corps and an advanced school for field musics was established at the Marine Barracks, Washington, D. C. This school was subsequently incorporated into the Field Music School at Parris Island, South Carolina.

During World War II a second Field Music School was established at San Diego, California and it remained in operation until 1965 when the reduced requirements for field musics made the operation of two schools uneconomical.

DRUM AND BUGLE CORPS

The United States Marine Drum and Bugle Corps, Marine Barracks, Washington, D.C., known as the "Commandant's Own" was formed in 1934 to augment the United States Marine Band and to perform independently at parades and ceremonies. Marine Corps combat commitments during World War II drew most of the musicians from the drum and bugle corps, making it temporarily inoperative. In 1946 the unit was reorganized with 17 men. These numbers gradually increased to 25 and remained at that level until 1956 when the unit received official designation as the "United States Marine Drum and Bugle Corps." At that time the current strength of 48 Marines was authorized. In 1957 the leader's rank was raised to Warrant Officer.

At present the United States Marine Drum and Bugle Corps makes more than 200 public appearances annually throughout the United States and overseas, performing at a variety of military ceremonies, civic functions, historical celebrations, sporting events and reunions of a local, national, and international nature.

Chapter 1

THE FIELD MUSIC BUGLER

1-1. GENERAL

    Commanders having an authorized drum and bugle corps may assign a bugler to serve as field music of the guard.

1-2. ROUTINE DUTIES

    a. A bugler assigned as the field music of the guard is subject to the general and special orders of the guard. His post is the guardhouse unless otherwise directed by the commanding officer. The duties of the field music of the guard are as follows:

        (1) <u>Sounding calls</u>. It is the direct responsibility of the field music of the guard to sound calls as prescribed by the commanding officer and when directed by the commander of the guard. In the absence of the drum and bugle corps, the field music sounds morning and evening colors.

        (2) <u>Ringing the ship's bell</u>. As a member of the guard, the field music may be assigned to ring the ship's bell. The proper method for sounding. The time is to strike the bell in groups of two, pausing slightly between each group; when an odd number of bells is prescribed the odd bell is counted as a group and is sounded last. The time/bell chart is as follows:

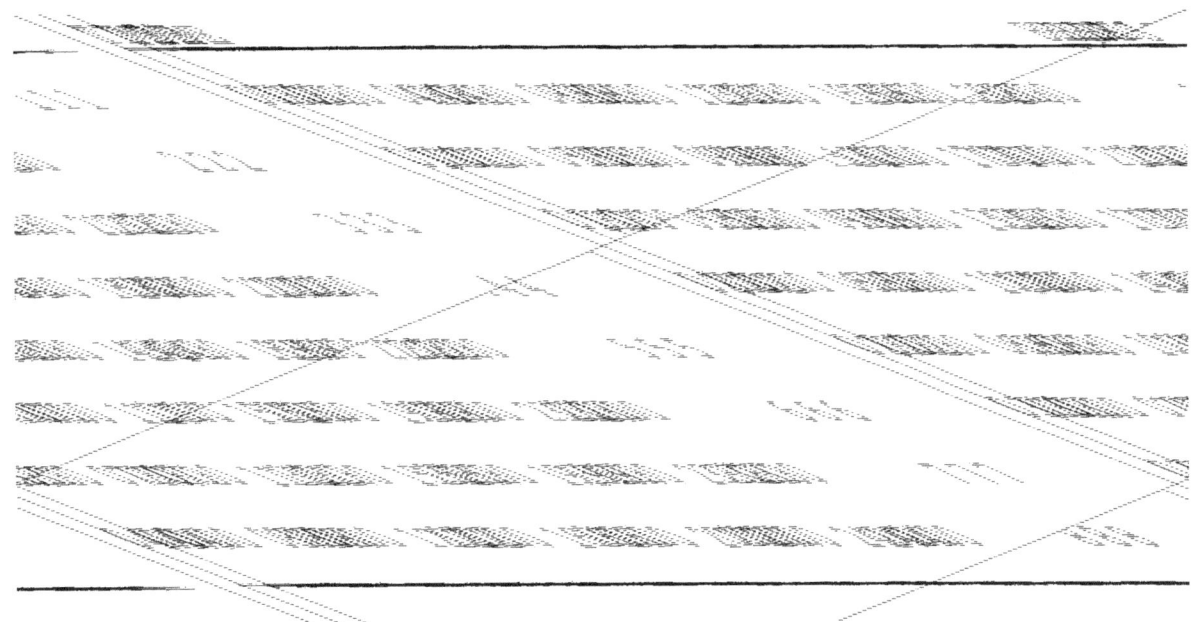

1-3. GUARD MOUNTS

In an informal guard mount the field music forms with the members of the guard and is inspected with the guard. In a formal guard mount the field music bugler forms on the parade field with the drum and bugle corps and is inspected with the musical unit. (Specific functions of the bugler during a guard mount are contained in the Landing Party Manual, Chapter 5, Section Iv.) Upon completion of the guard mount, the field music reports to the new sergeant of the guard.

1-4. FUNERALS

The bugler, when directed to serve as part of a funeral escort, reports to the escort commander, then places himself in the line of file closers. At the grave site, upon the commander's order to present arms, the bugler positions him-self at the head of the grave, facing the foot of the grave, and salutes until after the third rifle volley. The bugler then sounds Taps, salutes again, faces about and resumes his original position.

Chapter 2

THE BUGLE CALLS

2-1.   GENERAL

    a. Joseph Haydn, the celebrated musician, wrote the first bugle calls about 1793, but it was not until many years later that they were introduced into the military.

    b. The number of calls that a field music bugler is required to know has diminished since the first printing of this manual, due to changes which have occurred in the Marine Corps. For example, the calls, Stable Call and To Horse, are no longer used for obvious reasons, Also, since the Marine Corps no longer stations field musics aboard naval vessels, the calls that were used aboard these vessels are now obsolete.

2-2.   BASIC PERFORMANCE

    a. Bugle calls should conform to the music found in this chapter, as these are the only calls that are appropriate for the purposes indicated by the explanations that accompany each call. Particular attention must be given to rhythm, tempo, and intonation.

    b. Most calls are sound3d by one field music who, as a rule, is the Field Music of the Guard; however, such calls as Assembly, Reveille, Retreat, Adjutant's Call, and To the Color are sometimes sounded by the drum and bugle corps.

2-3.   PRECAUTIONS

    The following are precautions to avoid common errors in the execution of bugle calls and should be given additional consideration.

    a. Carry On. The eighth notes must be played evenly.

    b. First Call. The sixteenth-note groupings are not triplets. They should sound like the last three notes of a sextuplet.

    c. Guard Mounting. This call is written in 6/8 time, which is commonly beaten two beats per measure. Therefore, the first eighth- and sixteenth-note figuration in the sixth measure is played on the first downbeat and the same figuration in the third and eighth measures is played on the second downbeat.

d. <u>Tattoo</u>. The dotted quarter- and eighth-note figurations in the
1st and 5th measures must be executed properly; i.e., the eighth note
must be played exactly on the second upbeat of these two measures. The
dotted eighth- and sixteenth-note figuration on the fourth beat of the
12th measure should not be played as two eighth notes. The sixteenth
notes in the 17th and 18th measures should not be played as eighth notes
and the eighth notes in the 24th, 25th, and 26th measures should not be
played as sixteenth notes.

e. <u>Retreat</u>. The eighth notes in the 4th, 6th, and 12th measures are
played on the second upbeat of these measures.

2-4. BUGLE CALLS

The following 25 calls are a list of the bugle calls alphabetically.

1. <u>Adjutant's Call</u>.

Announces that the adjutant is about to form the guard,
battalion, or regiment. Immediately following the last note
of this call, the drum and bugle corps plays a march, and all
companies or details march on line. <u>Adjutant's Call</u> follows
<u>Assembly</u> at whatever interval the commanding officer prescribes.

2. <u>Assembly</u>.

Sounded as a signal for assembly of companies or details
at a designated place.

3. <u>Attention</u>.

Sounds as a signal for everyone to stand at attention
and maintain silence.

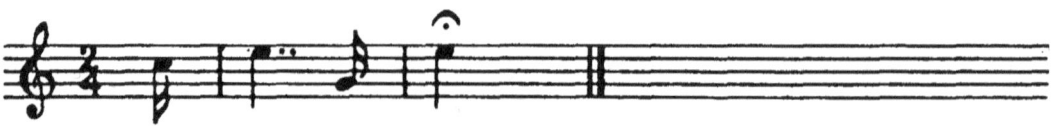

4. <u>Call to Quarters</u>.

Before the day or watches and clocks, this call was sounded 5 minutes before Taps as a signal for all men not on watch to go to their quarters. In modern times it is continued because of the tradition surrounding it and because of its beauty. Although post regulations vary, <u>Tattoo</u> is usually sounded at 2145, <u>Call to Quarters</u> at 2155, and <u>Taps</u> at 2200.

5. <u>Carry On</u>.

Sounded after <u>Attention</u> as a signal to return to whatever work or routine was carried on before <u>Attention</u> was sounded.

6. <u>Church Call</u>.

Sounded as a signal that divine services are about to be held. It may also be used to form a funeral escort.

7. <u>Fire Call</u>.

Sounded in case of fire, or fire drill, as a signal for general assembly and usually followed by one or more blasts (the number specified in fire orders) to designate the location of the fire. In garrison, it is customarily sounded inside the entrances of all buildings. The bugler then reports to the Officer of the Day.

8. <u>First Call</u>.

Sounded as a warning signal for a roll call formation and for all ceremonies except guard mounting. It is also sounded 5 minutes before <u>Morning Colors</u> and <u>Retreat</u> (<u>Evening Colors</u>). Depending upon regulations, the drum and bugle corps assessable 5 at <u>First Call</u>.

9. <u>First Call for Mess</u>.

Sounded as a warning call, 5 minutes before <u>Mess Call</u>.

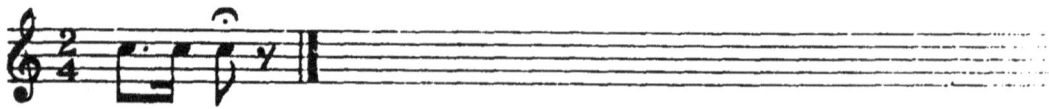

10. <u>First Sergeant's Call</u>.

Sounded as a signal for first sergeants to report to the adjutant or sergeant major with guard reports or for orders and instructions.

11. <u>Guard Mounting</u>.

Sounded as a signal to prepare for guard mount. It is followed by <u>Assembly</u>.

12. <u>Liberty Call</u>.

Sounded as a signal that men may leave the garrison or camp on authorized liberty.

13. <u>Mail Call</u>.

Sounded as a signal that mail is ready for distribution.

14. <u>Mess Call</u>.

   Sounded as a signal to assemble for chow breakfast, dinner, or supper.

15. <u>Officer's Call</u>.

   Sounded to notify all officers to report to the commanding officer. It is also used at other times to call all officers to assemble at a certain designated point.

16. <u>Pay Call</u>.

   Sounded to signal that the troops will be paid.

17. <u>Recall</u>.

   Sounded as a signal for certain duties to cease.

18. Retreat (Evening Colors).

      Sounded at all Marine barracks, camps, and naval stations, by a bugler or by the drum and bugle corps at sunset each day. The flag leaves the truck, or peak, at the first note of the music and is normally lowered slowly enough to reach the waiting guard on the last note of the music. This call is preceded by Attention and followed by Carry On. At Marine posts when an evening parade is held, and at naval stations when a band is present in formation, the flag is not lowered during the sounding of Retreat. In such cases the drum and bugle corps sounds Retreat, and immediately afterward the band plays the National Anthem, at the first note of which the flag leaves the truck or peak and is lowered slowly in time with the music. Evening Colors marks the end of the official day.

19. <u>Reveille</u>.

Sounded to awaken all men for morning roll call.

20. <u>Secure</u>.

Sounded after an exercise or drill as a signal to secure.

21. <u>Sick Call</u>.

Sounded, according to post regulations, as a signal for men requiring medical attention to report to the sick bay.

22. <u>Taps</u>.

   The last call at night. Sounded as a signal for all men to
retire and extinguish all lights except night lights. It is usually preceded at a prescribed interval by <u>Call to Quarters</u>. <u>Taps</u>
is also sounded at last honors to naval or military men being in-
terred.

   In 1862, General Daniel Butterfield, commander of a brigade
in the Civil War, composed the present bugle piece and directed
that it be substituted for the drum "taps." (Prior to that time,
the end of the day was signaled by striking three distinct blows,
or "taps," of the drum--hence the name "taps.") The first bugler
to play these solemn, beautiful notes was Oliver W. Norton, bugler
of General Butterfield's brigade, which at that time (July, 1862)
was encamped at Harrison's Landing, on the James River in Virginia.
3hortly thereafter the call was adopted by otht3r units in the
Federal Army and the Confederate Army.

23. <u>Tattoo</u>.

   This call is sounded in the evening as a signal to prepare
to retire.

24. <u>To the Color (Morning Colors)</u>.

    Sounded by the bugler or by the drum and bugle corps at 0800 each morning at all Marine barracks, camps, and naval stations. At the first note, the flag is quickly raised to the truck, or peak. This call is preceded by <u>Attention</u> and followed by <u>Carry On</u>.

    On occasions when the flag is to be flown at half-mast, it is raised as usual during the sounding of <u>To the Color</u>. Thereafter it is immediately lowered to half-mast, but such action is not part of the flag-raising ceremony.

25. <u>Echo Taps</u>.

    The requirement may arise occasionally for the sounding of <u>Echo Taps</u>. Two buglers are utilized, spaced an appropriate distance apart to simulate an echo.

Chapter 3

THE FIELD MUSIC DRUMMER

3-1. BACKGROUND

     The drums utilized by the Marine Corps drum and bugle corpshave under-
gone few changes through the years. The two most important innovations
were the plastic snare and batter heads introduced in 1937 and a new type
of snare unit introduced in 1967. Formerly, drumheads made of calfskin
were utilized; however, these were adversely affected by weather
conditions. In hot weather these heads would shrink and in damp or rainy
weather they would lose their tension, greatly reducing the quality of
sound produced by the drum. In addition, the calfskin had to be soaked
in water, tucked around a wooden hoop, and allowed to dry prior to being
secured to the drum shell. The plastic heads and metal hoops are an
integral unit, which makes replacing a drumhead a relatively simple
operation. Prior to the use of the present snare unit, the snare strands
were attached to the bottom side of the drum and stretched across the
snare or bottom head of the drum to the opposite side, where they were
again attached to the side of the drum. With this method, the pressure
of the snares against the head was uneven) i.e., the pressure was greater
at the ends of the snares than at the center. The snare unit on drums
now being utilized by Marine Corps drum and bugle corps is constructed as
one unit. The snares are contained within a rectangular frame, which
places the snares evenly against the snare head. This method allows even
pressure along the surface of the snare head. Additionally, each
individual strand is equipped with an adjusting screw, making it possible to adjust each strand to the same tension. This allows the snares to
vibrate in unison, giving the snare drum a fuller sound and more
projection.

3-2. GENERAL

     The percussion instatements presently in use in the Marine Corps are
the snare drum, tenor drum, Scotch bass drum, rudimental bass drum, timp-
toms. and cymbals (fig 3-1). The description of each is as follows:

     a. The parade snare drum. The parade snare drum is constructed of a
wooden, metal, or fiberglass cylindrical shell covered with a plastic
veneer or, in the case of the metal drum, chrome-plated. This shell is
generally 12 inches deep and 15 inches in diameter. The snare drum has
a batter (top) head and a snare (bottom) head, both usually made of
Mylar plastic, and insensitive to all but the most extreme weather conditions. Stretched across the snare head are from 10 to 18 individual
strands of wire, gut, nylon, or any combination of these depending on
the type of sound desired. These snares vibrate when the batter head is
struck, thereby giving the parade snare drum its characteristic crisp
buzzing sound.

     b. The tenor drum. The tenor drum is constructed basically the same
as the snare drum with the exception of the snares, which are eliminated,
and the size, which is generally slightly larger. The basic difference
in sound between the snare drum and the tenor drum is derived from the
elimination of the snares giving the tenor drum a hollow tom-tom sound
which blends in between the snare drum and the Scotch bass drum.

c.   The Scotch bass drum. Aside from the larger size, the Scotch bass drum is constructed the same as the tenor drum but instead of a top and bottom head, the Scotch bass drum has a large (26- to 30-inch-diameter) head on either side of a comparatively narrow (8- to 10-inch-ide) shell. The Scotch drum is used mainly to keep a steady marching tempo.

d.   The rudimental bass drum. Recently the Marine Corps has adopted a particular-sized drum called the rudimental bass drum. This drum provides a background accompaniment to the bugle section. More specifically it utilizes the rudiments of the snare and tenor drummer. The standard sizes for the rudimental bass drum are 14 by 26 inches and 12 by 24 inches. Rudimental bass drum mallets are used to help project the specific sound of this drum. The effects of this drum, both visual and sound, add considerably to the percussion section of the drum and bugle corps.

e.   The timp-toms. This is the latest instrument added to the percossion section of the drum and bugle corps within the Marine Corps. The timp-toms are actually three different-sized drums fastened together by a bracket that holds them in a triangular shape for ease of playing. The three drums may be individually tuned to produce three different tones. The sizes of the individual drums are as follows:

```
Tenor:     14 inches deep by 16, 18, or 20 inches in diameter
Baritone:  16 inches deep by 20, 22, or 24 inches in diameter
Bass:      16 inches deep by 24, 26, or 28 inches in diameter
```

The musical ranges of the various-sized drums are as follows:

	Size	Range
Tenor:	14" by 16"	F to A-flat
	14" by 18"	D to F
	14" by 20"	B to D
Baritone:	16" by 20"	A to C
	16" by 22"	C-flat to A
	16" by 24"	E-flat to C-flat
Bass:	18" by 24"	E-flat to C-flat
	18" by 26"	C to E-flat
	18" by 28"	A to C

The tonal expression of the timp-toms adds to the bugle section by tonal reinforcement and melodic accompaniment.

f.   The cymbals. The cymbals consist of two thin, slightly concave circular brass plates. The sound is gained by striking these plates together in a glancing manner. The sizes used by drum and bugle corps range from 14 to 25 inches in diameter depending on the depth of sound desired and, in the case of the larger cymbals, the experience and knowledge edge of the cymbal player. Cymbals may also be twirled, which adds greatly to the overall visual effect of the drum and bugle corps.

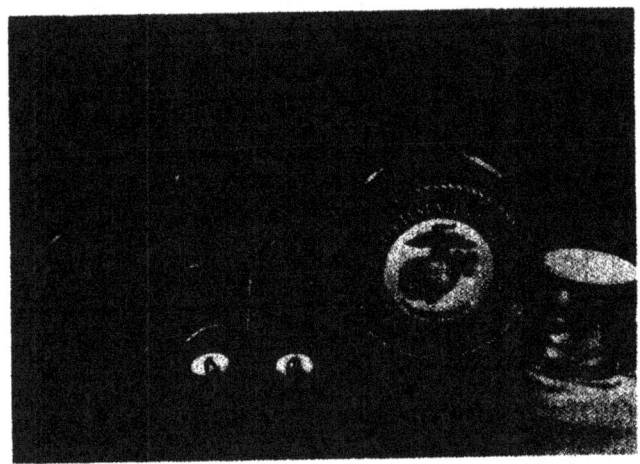

Fig. 3-1. The percussion instruments

3-3. CARE AND MAINTENANCE

a. <u>Shells</u>. The sun is probably the greatest cause of fading in drums covered with plastic veneer. A coat of good quality paste wax can be applied to the shell to help lessen this fading effect. The drums should also be kept in the shade as much as possible. For metal-shelled drums, a soft damp cloth may be used, followed by a dry cloth to keep them clean. The occasional application of a good quality metal polish is recommended.

b. <u>Hardware</u>. The metal parts of a drum are usually chrome- or nickel-plated and these parts may also be wiped with a soft damp cloth and immediately after, by a dry soft cloth. The occasional application of a good metal polish is also recommended.

c. <u>Heads</u>. Modern drumheads are made of plastic and need very little care and maintenance. However, the head may be cleaned with a damp cloth. The bead of the drumstick should be kept clean to avoid transfer of dirt and grime to the head. The changing of a broken or unserviceable head is a simple operation. You remove the rim from the shell by using a drum key. You must remove the old head and position a new head on the shell. Then you replace the rim and tighten the tension rods evenly. The proper method for tightening the tension rods is to alternate from one side of the drum to the opposite side until the proper tension is achieved.

3-4. PRACTICE PADS

A practice pad is usually a disk of rubber about 6 to 8 inches in diameter which is attached to a wooden or metal base inclined at an angle of about 30o. Currently in use within the Marine Corps is a new type of practice pad which is a great improvement over old types. This pad is actually a small narrow snare drum. The batter and snare heads are about 13 inches in diameter. The heads are separated by a thin metal disk with a foam rubber or plastic disk on the upper side. This pad is equipped with snares and can be fully adjusted for height and angle. This type of practice pad has the feel of an actual drum, but is comparatively noiseless; yet the drummer can detect his errors.

3-5. HOLDING THE SNARE DRUM STICKS

a. Left hand. Hold the stick in the hollow of the left hand, palm
up, 2/3 the distance from the striking end and midway between the thumb
and the first two fingers. Let it pass over the third finger between
the first and second joints, the thumb resting on the forefinger (fig
3-2).

b. Right hand. Hold the right stick, palm down, gripped between the
thumb and the second finger, the other fingers closed loosely around
the stick to guide it (fig 3-3).

c. Both hands. When held properly, the sticks form an angle of 90°,
the tips touching the center of the drumhead (fig 3-4).

Fig 3-2. Left hand

Fig 3-3. Right hand

Fig 3-4. Both hands

3-6. RUDIMENTS

a. The rudiments of drumming are the basic beat pattern8 which, when repeated1 combined, and used in conjunction with drumming routines, form much of the drum music. The rudiments are designated by definite names and numbers. For example, the single ratamacue is rudiment No. 13. To some extent, the names describe the beats; a single paradiddle (rudiment No. 19) consists of four beats, like the four syllables of the word pa-ra-did-dle.

b. When learning to beat the stroke rolls, you will find it necessary at first to count the number of beats until you become proficient and feel the rhythm, accent, and 8tyle of each individual roll. The 5-, 9-, and 13-stroke rolls are beaten from hand to hand. The 7-, 10-, 11-, and 15-stroke rolls start with the left hand and end with the right. For the purpose of practice and exercise, all rolls may be played from hand to hand. On the following pages are the standard 25 American rudiments.

1. <u>The long roll</u> (rudiment No. 1). Begin by making two hard strokes with the left hand followed by two hard strokes with the right hand; then continue, alternating from hand to hand, gradually beating faster and faster until the beats are closed in a smooth roll. During practice, to overcome the tendency to make the first beat of each hand heavier than the second beat, accent the second beat fry to make both beats with each hand even in volume and evenly spaced or timed. Start slowly, and pay strict attention to the manner of holding the sticks. Strive for freedom of the arms and flexibility of the wrists. Endeavor to keep the tips of the sticks within the 3-inch circle.

The long roll

As played

As Written

1-A.   <u>The single-stroke roll</u> (rudiment No. 1-A). This roll is performed by making one stroke with each hand, alternately, starting slowly and gradually beating faster and faster until maximum speed is attained.

The single-stroke roll (as played)

2. The 5-stroke roll (rudiment No.2). Begin by making two
    beats with the left hand followed by two beats with the right
    hand, then one hard stroke with the left. This is known as the
    left-hand 5-stroke roll. Alternate, starting with two rights
    followed by two lefts and then one hard stroke with the right.
    This is known as the right-hand 5-stroke roll. It is beaten
    from hand to hand with the last stroke of the long roll, and you
    gradually increase the speed until smooth and close execution
    is attained. This is the shortest of the double-stroke rolls.

The 5-stroke roll

As played

As written

3. The 7-stroke roll (rudizm3nt No. 3). Begin by making two
    beats with the left hand followed by two beats with the right,
    then two more with the left and a single accented stroke with
    the right.

The 7-stroke roll

As written

4. <u>The 9-stroke roll</u> (rudiment No.4). Like the 5-stroke roll,
    this one is played from hand to hand. When begun and finished
    with the left hand, it is known as the left-hand 9-stroke roll;
    when reversed, it is a right-hand 9-stroke roll.

The 9-stroke roll

As played

As written

5. <u>The 10-stroke roll</u> (rudiment No.5). Flay a left-hand 9-stroke
    roll and add an accented beat with the right hand. This roll
    has an accent on the ninth and tenth strokes and, like the 7-
    stroke, starts with the left hand and ends with the right.

The 10-stroke roll

As played

As written

6. <u>The 11-stroke roll</u> (rudiment No.6). Like the 7-stroke roll, this roll begins with the left hand and ends with an accented right.

The 11-stroke roll

As played

As written

7. <u>The 13-stroke roll</u> (rudiment No. 7). To learn this roll. follow instructions for beating the 5- or 9,-stroke roll.

The 13-stroke roll

As played

As written

8. <u>The 15-stroke roll</u> (rudiment No. 8). To learn this roll,
follow instructions for beating the 7- or 11-stroke roll.

The 15-stroke roll

As played

As written

9. <u>The flam</u> (rudiment No. 9). Hold the left stick 2 inches from
the drumhead and the right stick at chin level. Strike the
drumhead so that the left stick hits slightly before the right.
The left stick strikes a very light tap and the right a hard
blow. This beat is called a right-hand flam. Reverse the
position of the sticks and use the same procedure for a left-
hand flam. Continue alternating the position of the sticks.

The flam

As played

As written

10. The ruff (rudiment No. 10). Hold the sticks in the same man-
    ner as is making the flam. Make two left strokes and follow
    with a hard right stroke; then, alternate the position of the
    sticks and make two rights followed by a hard left. The first
    two strokes of each ruff sound lighter than the finishing
    strokes. This beat, like the flam, is from hand to hand.

The ruff

As played

As written

11. The single drag (rudiment No. 11). Make two strokes with the
    left hand and one with the right, followed by one hard stroke
    with the left. Then reverse the position of the sticks and
    make two strokes with the right, one with the left, followed
    by a hard right.

The single drag

As played

As written

12. The double drag (rudiment No. 12). Make two strokes with the left hand and one with the right, then two with the left and one with the right, followed by a hard left. Reverse the position of the sticks and make two strokes with the right and one with the left, then two with the right and one with the left, and follow with a hard right.

The double drag

As played

As written

13. The single ratamacue (rudiment No. 13). The single ratamacue is frequently used with the single and double drags.

The single ratamacue

As played

As written

14. <u>The double ratamacue</u> (rudiment No. 14). The double and triple ratamacue are frequently used in playing "fancy beats" in quickstep time.

The double ratamacue

As played

As written

15. <u>The triple ratamacue</u> (rudiment No. 15).

The triple ratamacue

As played

As written

16.   <u>The flam accent</u> (rudiment No. 16). Begin by making a right-
       hand flam followed by a left stroke and a right stroke; then
       a left-hand flam followed by a right stroke and a left stroke.
       <u>Accent the flam.</u>

Flam accent

17.   <u>The flamacue</u> (rudiment No. 17). Make a right-hand flam followed
       by a left stroke, then a right stroke, a left stroke, and an-
       other right-hand flam. Accent the stroke following the flam.
       (This beat is not played from hand to hand.)

The flamacue

18.   <u>The flam tap</u> (rudiment No. 18). Make a right-hand flam followed
       by a right stroke; then a left-hand flam followed by a left stroke.

The flam tap

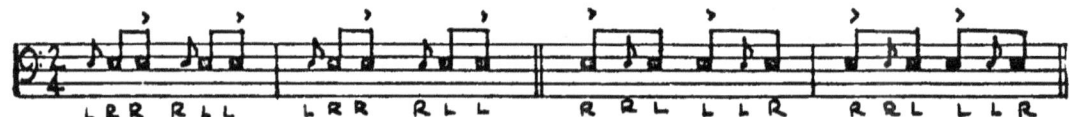

19. <u>The singe paradiddle</u> (rudiment No. 19). Make a right stroke, a left stroke, and two rights; then a left stroke, a right stroke, and two lefts. Accent as indicated below.

The single paradiddle

20. <u>The double paradiddle</u> (rudiment No. 20). Accent as indicated below.

The double paradiddle

As played

As written

21. <u>The flam paradiddle</u> (rudiment No. 21). This rudiment is similar to the single paradiddle except that instead of the accented
stroke it begins with a flam. Thus: flam, left, right, right;
then reverse: flam, right, left, left; Beat from hand to hand.

The flam paradiddle

As written

22. <u>The flam paradiddle-diddle</u> (rudiment No. 22). This rudiment is
similar to the double paradiddle except that instead of the accented
stroke it begins with a flam. Thus: flam, left, right, right,
left, left; then reverse: flam, right, left, left, right, right.
Beat from hand to hand.

The flam paradiddle-diddle

As played

As written

23. <u>Drag Paradiddle No. 1</u> (rudiment No. 23). Begin with a right stroke and follow by a left-hand ruff, then a left and two right strokes; reverse and make a left-stroke, a right-hand ruff, a right and two lefts. Accent the stroke preceding the ruff. Beat from hand to hand.

Drag paradiddle No. 1

As played

As written

24. <u>Drag paradiddle No.2</u> (rudiment No. 24). This rudiment has two ruffs following the first stroke (instead of one ruff, as in drag paradiddle No. 1). Make a right stroke, two left-hand ruffs, a left and two rights; then reverse and make a left stroke, two right-hand ruffs, a right and two lefts. Accent the stroke preceding the two ruff 8.

Drag paradiddle No. 2

As played

As written

25. Rudiment No. 25: This rudiment is frequently used in marches.
Make a left-hand ruff, a left-hand stroke, and a right stroke.

Rudiment No. 25 (as played)

As played

As written

3-7. CARRIAGE OF THE DRUM

   a. Standing. The tendency while standing with the snare drum or tenor
drum is to lean to the right to compensate for the weight of the drum. If
the drummer stands in a natural position, the drum sling will hold the
drum in place.

   b. Marking time. Marking time is done by lifting the left leg about
2 inches off the deck. The left knee is not bent, thereby keeping the
drum as stable as possible.

   c. Marching. While marching, march as smoothly as possible. Do not
lean forward or backward; and march in a straight line.

Chapter 4

THE DRUM AND BUGLE CORPS

4-1. FIELD Military MUSIC SECTION

     On 15 January 1971 the Commandant of the Marine Corps established the
Field Military Music Section within the G-1 Division, Headquarters Marine
Corps. The mission of this section is to support the Assistant Chief of
Staff, G-1 in the administration and coordination of his staff cognizance
over all matters concerning Marine Corps Band and Marine Corps Drum and
Bugle Corps Units. These matters include organization, training, inspection, supply, personnel procurement, job description, personnel assign-
ments, tables of organization, table of allowances, assignment and employ-
ment of band and drum and bugle corps units and are addressed in coordination with other Headquarters Marine Corps staff agencies.

4-2. GENERAL

     a. The drum and bugle corps has become an integral part of the
Marine Corps. It increases morale and esprit de corps, furnishing
the commanding officer and his command a vital link to ceremonial
traditions.

     b. The function of the drum and bugle corps is to furnish appro-
priate music for military formations, street parades, social functions,
and entertainment; and to perform such other duties as may be directed
by the commanding officer.

4-3. BUGLES OF THE DRUM AND BUGLE CORPS

     a. Background. As drum and bugle corps came into existence within
the Marine Corps, the need for a more versatile bugle was apparent. The
Garrison or G bugle tuned in the key of G was capable of producing only
seven musical tones. This was adequate for all bugle calls, but greatly
limited the musical capabilities of a drum and bugle corps. As a result,
the C-D bugle, of which there were three types, the soprano, French horn,
and baritone, was adopted for use with Marine Corps drum and bugle corps.
The C-D bugle is essentially the G bugle with an added section of tubing
pitched in the key of D and controlled by a piston-type valve. With this
bugle the playing of a complete major scale was possible. In the early
1950's, a movable slide, similar to the trombone slide, was added to the
U-D bugle. With this slide, any given note could be lowered one-half
step making a full chromatic scale possible. Shortly thereafter, another
valve, the rotary valve, was utilized in lieu of the movable slide.
Although the rotary valve did not add to the musical tones available on
the G-D bugle with slide, it did greatly facilitate the half-step change.
The three original types of C-D bugles are similar in that they all have
the same musical tones available. However, the French horn and baritone
bugles are pitched one octave below the soprano bugle. The French horn
bugle is similar in tone to the band French horn, and the baritone bugle

corresponds with the band baritone horn. In 1957, the baritone bugle was replaced with the bass-baritone bugle. Both bugl3s have the same musical range; however, the bass-baritone is more resonant. Between 1964 and 1967, two new types of bugles were added to the drum and bugle corps. These were the mellophone and contra-bass bugles. The mellophone, as the name implies, has a mellow tone, and is in the same range as the French horn bugle. The contra-bass bugle became the lowest-pitched instrument in a drum and bugle corps, being pitched one octave below the bass-baritone bugle. These two instruments added significantly to the musical range and capabilities of the drum and bugle corps.

    b. <u>Types of bugles</u>. Five type of bugles are commonly in use in Marine Corps drum and bugle corps today: the <u>soprano</u>, <u>French horn</u>, <u>mellophone</u>, <u>bass-baritone</u>, and <u>contra-bass</u> bugles (fig 4-i). These five types of bugles are divided into two groups: the G-D bugles, and the newer and more versatile G-F bugles. Toe Marine Corps presently is changing to the G-F bugles, due mainly to their ability to play the A and the F in the octave below tuning C--notes which are of great value musically but which are impossible to play on the G-D bugle with the rotary valve.

    (1) <u>Sopranos</u>. The soprano bugle has a range of approximately two and a half octaves starting with the F-sharp below middle C. The notes within its range, that cannot be played on this bugle are:

        C-D bugles: A-flat, A, B-flat, below middle C, and
                    E-flat, E, F, A-flat, A, below tuning C.

        G-F bugles: F-sharp, C, A-flat, A, below middle C, and
                    C-sharp, D, E-flat, A-flat, below tuning C.

    (2) <u>French horn</u>. The French horn bugle has the same range as the soprano, but is pitched one octave below the soprano.

    (3) <u>Mellophone</u>. The mellophone bugle has the same range and pitch as the French horn bugle; however, due to the size of its bell and the manner of its construction, this bugle has a more mellow tone.

    (4) <u>Bass-baritone</u>. The bass-baritone bugle has the same range and pitch as the French horn; however, due to its larger tubing, the bass-baritone is normally played in the lower portion of its range.

    (5) <u>Contra-bass</u>. This bugle has the same range as the bass-baritone, but is pitched one octave lower, which makes it the lowest pitched bugle of the five types in use within the Marine Corps.

C. Care and maintenance

   (1) Cleaning. All bugles should be cleaned at least once a week,
       by the following method: (1) Run warm, soapy water through
       all tubing and clean with a flexible cleaning brush. (2) Rinse
       the bugle well to remove all traces of soap. (3) Wipe the
       bugle with a soft cloth or chamois. (4) Apply petroleum
       jelly to all slides, and valve oil to the valve and the rotary
       valve. The most important part of the bugle to be kept clean,
       and the most neglected, is the mouthpiece. Glean this with
       warm or hot soapy water, using a mouthpiece brush. The inside
       or bore of the mouthpiece should shine. Take care to avoid
       denting the rim of the mouthpiece. Also, avoid playing on a
       mouthpiece which has the silver or nickel plating worn off;
       this could very easily lead to brass poisoning.

   (2) Maintenance. All major repairs should be handled by a compe-
       tent instrument repair man. However, all drum and bugle corps
       should have a mouthpiece puller available and personnel should
       be able to use it properly.

   (3) Care. The best method of caring for a bugle is by preventive
       maintenance. Keep the bugle, particularly the mouthpiece,
       valves, and slides clean and properly greased and oiled.

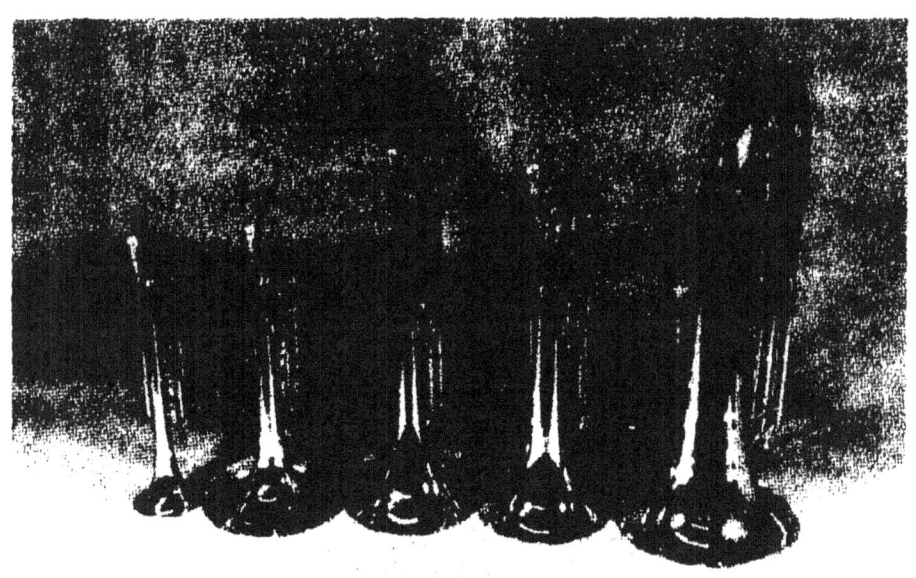

Fig 4-1. Types of bugles

4-4. POSITIONS OF THE BUGLES

a. General. The following positions are given as guidelines. Various positions may be used to achieve a desired effect; however, it must be kept in mind that all positions should be uniform, and the movement to these positions must be made sharply, in unison, and in a military manner.

b. Attention. The bugler, with the exception of the contra-bass bugler, is in the prescribed position of Attention with the bugle held in his right hand. His right arm is bent so that the bugle is belt-high, perpendicular to his body, and parallel to the deck. The mouthpiece is facing toward the front (fig 4-2). The contra-bass bugler holds his bugle cradled in both arms at an angle of about 450 with the mouthpiece to his left (fig 4-3).

(1) First variation. The bugle, except the contra-bass, is held in the right hand. The right arm is extended downward with the bugle perpendicular to the deck, and in line with the right leg. The mouthpiece is upward (fig 4-4).

(2) Second variation. This position is the same as the first variation except the bugle is held at an angle of about 300. The mouthpiece is facing forward.

(3) Third variation. The bugle is held about 4 inches from the bugler1s chest, parallel with his body, and perpendicular to the deck. The mouthpiece is facing upward (fig 4-5).

c. Parade Rest. The bugler is in the pres3ribed position of Parade Rest. The bugle is held with the hands side by side, lowered to arm's length, and parallel to the deck. The mouthpiece is facing to the bugler's left (fig 4-6).

d. Playing. The bugle is held to the players lips, parallel with the deck, and perpendicular to the body. The hands are placed in the most convenient position to facilitate the operation of both the valve and the rotary valve (fig 4-7).

e. Inspection. The position of Inspection is the same as the third variation of Attention (fig 4-5).

Fig 4-2. Attention

Fig 4-3. Attention, contra-bass

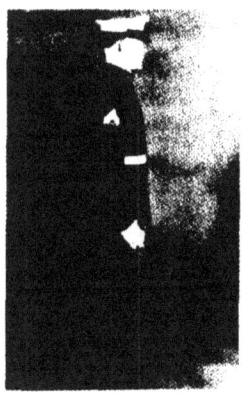

Fig 4-4. First variation

Fig 4-5. Third variation

Fig 4-6. Parade Rest

Fig 4-7. Playing

4-5. POSITIONS OF THE DRUMS

    a. General. The following positions (b-r below) are given as guide-
lines. Various positions may be used to achieve a desired effect; however, it must be kept in mind that all positions should be uniform, and
the movement to these positions must be made sharply, in unison, and in
a military manner.

    b. Attention (snare. tenor. and timp-toms). The drummer is at the
prescribed position of Attention. The drumsticks are held together in
both hands. The left hand is resting on the upper rim of the drum,
while the right hand is elevated slightly to keep the drumsticks parallel to the deck. The left palm is upward and the right palm facing the
drum(fig 4-8).

    c. Attention (Scotch bass and rudimental bass). The drummer is at
the prescribed position of Attention. The drumsticks are held in a
vertical position. The hands are resting on either side of the lower
portion of the drum rims (fig 4-9).

    d. Attention (cymbals). The cymbalist is in the prescribed position
of Attention with the arms extended along the sides. The cymbals are
held parallel with the body and perpendicular to the deck. The concave
sides are inboard (fig 4-10).

    e. Parade Rest (snare. tenor. and timp-toms). The drummer is in
the prescribed position of Parade Rest. The right hand grasps both
sticks, bringing them to the center of the body. The left hand moves
in position to cover the right hand. Both hands are resting on the upper rim of the drum (fig 4-11).

    f. Parade Rest (Scotch bass and rudimental bass). The drummer is at
the prescribed position of Parade Rest. The hands and sticks are in the
same position as described for Attention.

    g. Parade Rest (cymbals). The cymbalist is in the prescribed posi-
tion of Parade Rest. The cymbals are held in the same position as described for Attention.

    h. Prepare To Play (snare. tenor. and timp-toms).

        (1) First count. The first count of Prepare To Play is the same
             as the position described for Attention.

        (2) Second count. The drummer moves his right arm to a position
             900 to the width of his body. His elbow is at a 900 angle,
             with the stick held in the vertical position. His left hand
             is moving slightly to position the bead of the stick in the
             center of the batter head. Both hands move simultaneously
             (fig 4-12).

i. Prepare To Play (Scotch bass and rudimental bass). This position is the same as described for Attention. However, the bead of the mallets are moved approximately 3 inches from the surface of the drumheads (fig 4-13).

j. Prepare To Play (cymbals). The cymbalist is at the prescribed position of Attention except the cymbals are brought forward and upward to a position about 4 inches from the chest and about 12 inches apart (fig 4-14).

k. Inspection (snare and tenor). Both drumsticks are grasped in the right hand. The left hand moves downward and grasps the lower rim of the drum. The right hand simultaneously grasps the same side of the upper rim and the drum is rotated to a position centered on the belt, with the batter and snare heads facing outboard (fig 4-15).

l. Inspection (timp-toms). This position is the same as that of Attention.

m. Inspection (Scotch bass and rudimental bass). This position is the same as that of Attention.

n. Inspection (cymbals). The cymbalist is at the prescribed position of Attention. The cymbals are held at arms length, to the front of the body, at waist level, and are parallel to the deck and perpendicular to the body (fig 4-16).

o. Secure (snare and tenor). The drummer is at the prescribed position of Attention. His right hand grasps both sticks and his right arm is lowered to hang naturally at his side. His left hand grasps the lower rim directly below the sling attachment and rotates the drum to the left side of his body. The drum shell is held in the horizontal position with his left hand (fig 4-17).

p. Secure (timp-toms). This po8ition is the same as that Of Attention.

q. Secure (Scotch bass and rudimental bass). The drummer is at the prescribed position of Attention. His right hand grasps both sticks and his right arm is lowered to hang naturally at his aids. The right sling swivel is unhooked and the drum is grasped at the right upper rim with his left hand and rotated to his left side. The drum shell is held in the horizontal position with his left hand (fig 4-18).

r. Secure (cymbals). This position is the same as that of Attention.

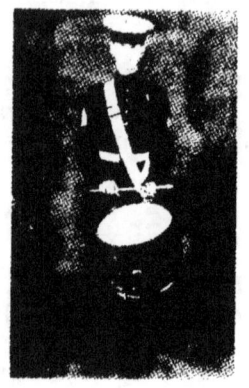

Fig 4-8

Fig 4-9

Fig 4-10

Fig 4-11

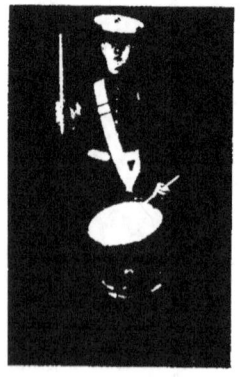

Fig 4-12

Fig 4-13

Fig 4-14

Fig 4-15

Fig 4-16

Fig 4-17

Fig 4-18

4-6. FORMATIONS

   a. <u>Marching unit</u>. As a marching unit for ceremonies, parades and other functions, two primary factors are to be considered: (1) sound, and (2) appearance. An efficient blending of both, proficiently executed, will produce a successful drum and bugle corps.

   b. <u>Alinement</u>. The alinements in playing formation are maintained as prescribed for an infantry unit with the following exceptions:

     (1) Left hands are not placed on the hips in dressing.

     (2) Intervals are obtained from the direction of the base file at 60 inches.

     (3) Rear-rank men cover their file leaders at 60 inches.

     (4) when marching in playing formation, the center or right-of-center file is the guide.

     (5) In playing formation at a halt, the drum major may command COVER IN FILE, and verify the intervals and alinement of files from a point 2 paces in front of each file prior to giving the command for and verifying the alinement of each rank.

   c. <u>Marching formation</u>. Formations may vary somewhat; however, the normal placement of personnel and the correct instrumentation for the standard 25-piece drum and bugle corps are given below:

	DM		
SN	SN	TN	TN
CY	1S	1S	SC
1S	1S	1S	2S
3S	3S	MP	2S
1B	FH	FH	2B
1B	1B	CB	2B

Key:

SN Snare drum	1S - 1st soprano	MP - Mellophone
TN - Tenor drum	2S - 2d soprano	1B - 1st bass baritone
Sc - Scotch drum	35 - 3d soprano	2B - 2d bass baritone
CY - Cymbals	FH - French horn	CB - Contrabass baritone
DM - Drum major		

   d. Inspections. The drum and bugle corps is inspected in
accordance with Marine Corps drill regulations. Normally,
the drum and bugle corps is formed in a column of fours in
marching formation. At the command PREPARE FOR INSPECTION,
the drum major verifies the alinement of the drum and bugle
corps and places himself, facing to the front, in the center
and 3 paces in front of the front rank. As the inspecting
officer approaches, the drum major faces about, calls the
drum and bugle corps to attention, faces to the front and
renders the baton salute. After the drum major has been inspected, the inspection is made from right to left in the
front and from left to right in the rear of each rank.

4-7. MOVEMENTS

a. <u>Facing</u>. Left, right, and about face will be executed as is pre-scribed in regulations.

b. <u>Turns, right and left</u>. On the drum major1s signal, the man on the right (left) flank of the front rank executes a right (left) flank movement. The signal of execution is given on the foot of the new direction (right foot for right turn, left foot for left turn). After executing the right (left) flank movement, the pivot man marches in the new direction for a distance equal to the depth of the drum and bugle corps(fig 4-19).

<u>Example</u>: The drum and bugle corps is 6 ranks deep; therefore there are 10 paces from the front rank to the rear rank; the pivot man steps off 10 paces in the new direction at a 30-inch pace. By moving in the new direction in this manner, all of the drum and bugle corps will be able to execute the turn at a full step. There will be no "half-stepping" around the pivot point. The pivot man commences a half-step after executing the above. The remainder of the front rank continues to march directly ahead, turning in the following manner: The second man in from the right (left) flank takes 2 additional forward paces after the signal of execution and then executes a right (left) flank movement; the third man in from the right (left) flank takes 2 additional paces forward past the point there the second man has turned 4 paces past the execution signal; this procedure is carried out throughout the remainder of the front rank until all men have made the flanking movement. As each member of the front rank comes in line with the flank (pivot) man, a half-step is commenced. When making turns, the rank guide shifts from the center (or right of center) column to the pivot column (right column on a right turn and the left column on a left turn). The remainder of the drum and bugle corps will follow along in kind. When the drum and bugle corps has completed the turn and is properly aliened, the drum major will signal FORWARD). The rank guide returns to the center column after stepping off with the normal 30-inch pace.

c. <u>Countermarch</u>. When the drum major gives the signal to counter-march (the signal of execution being given on the right foot), the front rank marches forward 4 paces and executes two successive right-flank movements commencing on the 5th pace (the left foot). The re-mainder of the ranks follow in kind, turning where the front rank has turned(fig 4-20). This movement is executed at the normal pace.

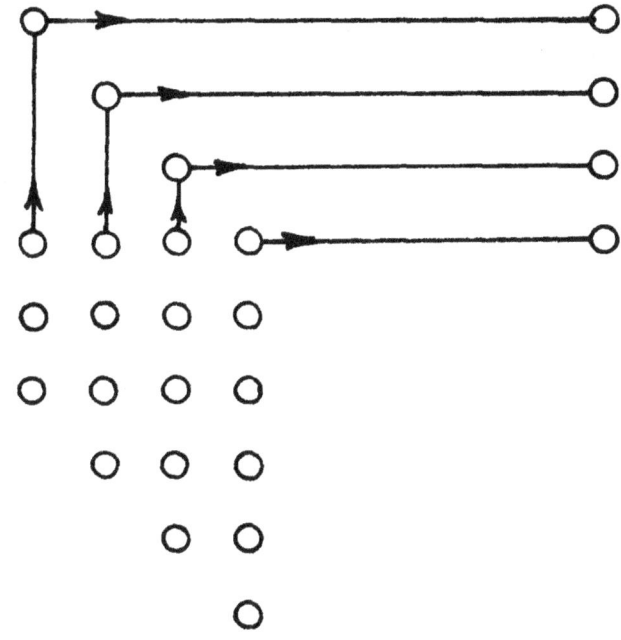

Fig 4-19

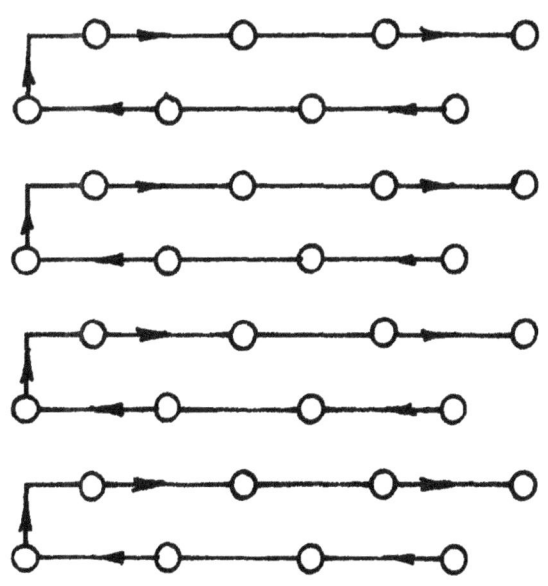

Fig 4-20

4-8. CEREMONIES

a. <u>General</u>. The various types of ceremonies in which a drum and bugle corps participates (i.e., reviews, presentations of decorations, ceremonial parades, street parades, escort of honor, guard mounting, funerals, and memorial services) are detailed in the Landing Party Manual. However, commanding officers frequently modify formations for ceremonies when the nature of the ground or exceptional circumstances require that such changes be made.

b. <u>Honors</u>. Certain Government officials, foreign dignitaries, and officers of flag rank are rendered appropriate "Honors" as prescribed by Navy Regulations. Such honors consist of ruffles and flourishes followed by either a march or <u>To the Color</u>; or, if the instrumentation of the drum and bugle corps is adequate, the national anthem may be played.

4-9. EXHIBITION DRILL

a. <u>General</u>. The performance of an exhibition drill is the primary function and concern of a drum and bugle corps in the entertaining phase of its mission. The degree of difficulty of the drill and music will depend on the proficiency of the musicians.

b. <u>Format</u>. As a guideline, the following format may be used.

(1) <u>Fanfare</u>. The exhibition drill should be started with a fanfare to gain the attention of the audience prior to the actual marching.

(2) <u>First musical selection</u>. This selection may be a march or popular-type selection. The time signature can be 2/4, 2/2, 4/4, 6/8 or, in rare cases, 3/4.

(3) <u>Drum solo</u>. Between each musical selection is a drum solo. This is used not only to position the drum and bugle corps for the next selection, but also to give buglers a short rest period. This drum solo is usually 32 counts in length and is followed by an 8-count rolloff to bring the bugles to the position L)f Prepare To Play in readiness for the next musical selection.

(4) <u>Second musical selection</u>. The same guidelines may be used as in the first selection, keeping in mind the need for variety. This selection can lead into a concert formation or a drum solo may be used to position the drum and bugle corps in a concert formation

(5) Concert. The musical selection for the concert is one of the high points of the drill. It is generally somewhat longer than the selections used on the march. It is usually a *production" type selection, possibly from a motion-picture sound track or a Broadway musical. Since the unit is not marching, the tempo may vary as necessary to achieve the desired effect. Patriotic selections are most appropriate for inclusion in the concert.

(6) Third and fourth musical selections. These also follow the guidelines of the first two selections. Again, variety is the main concern.

(7) Ending. It is appropriate and desirable for a marine Corps drum and bugle corps to end an exhibition drill with the Marines Hymn. A variation of this may be the playing of an ending selection and marching from the drill area in a parade formation, playing the Marines Hymn.

c. Additional guidelines.

(1) Length of drill. An average time for an exhibition drill is 12 minutes.

(2) Tempo. The tempo of the music played while drilling should fall between 128 and 132 beats per minute. There may be exceptions to this, such as the use of a slow march routine.

(3) Alignment and pace. The two singularly, most important considerations in an exhibition drill are alinement (or dress), which must be maintained, and the size of the pace used. The size of the pace should conform to the Marine Corps standard of 30 inches.

(4) Precision. All movements must be made with precision, in unison, and in a military manner.

Chapter 5

MANUAL OF THE BATON

5-1. GENERAL

      The drum major1s baton is used to convey commands (signals) to the
drum and bugle corps while in formation. The components of the baton are
the ball, the staff, the ferrule, and the cord and tassels. The drill
used in training the drum major in the execution of the baton signals
is known as the manual of the baton. The following paragraphs describe
the phases of this manual.

NOTE: When marching at secure instruments, oral commands will be used.

5-2. POSITIONS OF THE BATON

   a.   Order baton. The position assumed by the drum major while the
drum and bugle corps is at the halt is called order baton (fig 5-1).
This position is executed in one count as follows:

      (1) The right hand grasps the staff near the ball so that the back
          of the hand is to the front. The ferrule is placed on the line
          with, and touching the right center of, the right shoe. The
          right arm is extended diagonally down and to the side of the
          body at an angle of approximately 45.

      (2) The left hand is placed on the hip at the waist line, fingers
          extended to the front and joined, thumb to the rear, wrist
          straight, the elbow on a line with the body.

{li 2643_090.GIF:FIG 5-1 ORDER BATON}

Fig 5-1. Order baton.

b. <u>Baton twirl</u>. The baton twirl is a forward circular motion of the baton designed to attract the attention of the members of the unit in order that they may be prepared for the baton signal to follow. When practicable, the twirl should precede all preparatory signals.

    (1) <u>Starting position</u>. To assume the starting position of the twirl, the drum major swings the ferrule in an arc upward and back so that the staff rests on the arm midway between the shoulder and the elbow. The staff is at an angle of 450 (fig 5-2&).

    (2) <u>The twirl</u>. To execute the twirl, the drum major holds the baton firmly in the crotch of the hand between the first finger and thumb, fingers supporting the staff loosely. By moving the wrist downward and inward, the staff will traverse a circle to the outside of the right arm; the ball will traverse a circle between the right hand and the body. The elbow is held loosely to the side of the body in a vertical line with the shoulder, the forearm forward and to the right and sufficiently raised to cause the ferrule to clear the ground. Twirls should be executed rhythmically in two counts (fig 5-2B).

A. Starting Position.   B. The Twirl.

Fig 5-2.   Baton twirl.

C. Carry baton. The position in which the baton is held by the drum major when marching and not marking cadence is known as carry baton. This position is executed as follows:

(1) The staff is held near the ball with the right hand, with the ball alongside the right leg, the ferrule up, staff resting against the front of the right arm (fig 5-3).

(2) The position of the left arm is the same as prescribed in paragraph 5-2a(2) or may be allowed to swing as in marching.

Fig 5-3. Carry baton.

d. <u>Port baton</u>. To assume the port baton position, bring the wrist
and arm 6 inches in front of the chest, holding the baton diagonally
across the body with the ferrule up and to the right (fig 5-4)

Fig 5-4. Port baton.

e.   Cadence baton. To establish the proper cadence of a march while the drum and bugle corps is marching and playing, or to correct discrepancies in tempo, the drum major may execute a movement known as cadence baton, This movement, initiated from port baton, is executed in two counts as follows:

   (1) From port baton, the baton is raised diagonally upward and to the right center (fig 5-5).

   (2) The cadence is indicated by returning the baton to port baton on the first beat and to the position as described in (1) above on the second beat.

Fig 5-5.   Cadence baton.

f. Baton salute. The baton salute is executed as follows:

(1) From order baton:

(a) Raise the right arm upward and forward, fully extended, to a horizontal position.

(b) By bending the right arm at the elbow, carry the baton horizontally to the left so that the back of the hand is touching the left shoulder, arm remaining horizontal (fig 5-6). Return to order baton, through the reverse of these movements.

(2) From carry baton and cadence baton:

(a) Bring the baton from the carry or cadence position to the starting position of the twirl.

(b) Execute the twirl and, at the completion of the twirl, extend the arm and baton outward and downward to a 450 angle. Execute the movement as prescribed in f(1)(b) above and return to the respective baton position, omitting the twirl.

Fig 5-6. Baton salute.

g. <u>Parade rest</u>. Swing the ferrule up and to the left, keeping the right arm stationary. When the baton reaches the horizontal position, the left hand grasps the baton, back of the hand to the front, left arm extended at the left side. Simultaneously, the left foot is moved smartly 12 inches to the left. This position may be used when the unit is at ease or rest (fig 5-7).

Fig 5-7. Parade rest.

5-3. BATON SIGNALS

a. <u>General</u>. The baton signal is the visible counterpart of the oral
command and, as such, should be executed with rhythm, precision, and deci-
siveness. The drum major will execute all baton signals while facing
front unless otherwise indicated.

b. <u>Prepare to play</u>. The baton signal for <u>Prepare to play</u> is executed
as follows:

    (1) <u>Preparatory signal</u>. The baton is brought to <u>Port Baton</u> then
         lowered smartly (fig 5-8) keeping the same angle signaling the
         performers to bring their instruments into position for play-
         ing.

    (2) <u>Signal of execution</u>. The baton is fully extended overhead and
         to the right at a 450 angle from the horizontal signaling the
         position <u>Prepare to play</u>.

Fig 5-8. Prepare to play.

c.   _Downbeat_. The baton signal for the downbeat is executed as follows:

   (1)   The baton is fully extended upward and slightly to the right of center, as prescribed in b(2).

   (2)   The downbeat is executed from the position described in (1) above by moving the baton in a small arc to the left and upward, followed in cadence by a decisive return of the baton to the port position.

d.   _Play softly_. This command, executed while playing at the halt or marching, may be executed facing the unit.

   (1)   The baton is extended skyward, ball up, ferrule in front of the waist (fig 5-9). Execute and terminate this signal at phrase endings if possible.

Fig 5-9. Play softly.

e. "Cutoff." The cutoff, signal to the drum and bugle corps to cease playing, is executed as follows:

  (1) Preparatory signal. The baton, grasped at the ball with the right hand, is fully extended to a position overhead, slightly to the right of center (fig 5-bA).

  (2) Signal of execution. At the count of "one" the baton is carried to the left (fig 5-10B); at the count of "two" it is returned slightly to the right (fig 5-10G); and at the count of "three" it is lowered to the position Port Baton.

The baton movements described in subparagraph (1) and (2) above, executed in cadence, direct the drum and bugle corps to cease playing on the third count. When practicable, the cutoff should be executed at the completion of a phrase.

A. Preparatory signal

B. Signal of execution (first motion)

C. Signal of execution (second motion)

Fig 5-10. Cutoff.

f. Mark time. The baton is held horizontal by both hands, slightly in front of the body, arms on line with forehead. This signal is executed while facing the unit (fig 5-11).

Fig 5-1. Mark time.

g. <u>Prepare to Mark Time, from position of Halt while playing</u>. This signal consists of two positions of one count each. The preliminary position is the same as for mark time. Fingers may be closed or extended (fig 5-11).

(1)   On count "one" (executed on the weak beat, or right foot), lower the baton smartly, keeping it horizontal, grasped by both hands, to a position with arms fully extended downward (fig 5-12).

(2)   On count "two" (executed on the strong beat, or left foot), raise the baton to preliminary position. On this count, the drum major and unit commence marking time simultaneously with the movement. This signal is executed while facing the unit.

Fig 5-12. Prepare to Mark Time, From the Halt while playing.

h. <u>Halt</u>. This signal consists of four positions of one count each. The preliminary position is the same as <u>mark time</u>.

(1) On count "one" (executed on the strong beat or left foot), lower the right arm to a shoulder-high position, keeping the left arm extended. The baton is now at a 450 angle, ball down (fig 5-13A).

(2) On count "three" (executed on the weak beat or right foot), lower the left arm to a shoulder-high position, the right hand remaining at shoulder height. The baton becomes horizontal (fig 5-13B).

(3) On count "three" (executed on the strong beat or left foot), extend both arms, baton horizontal, as in the preliminary movement of mark time.

(4) On count "four" (executed on the weak beat or right foot), lower the baton smartly, keeping it horizontal, arms fully extended downward, at approximately hip height. This signal is executed while facing the unit.

A.   B.

Fig 5-13.   Halt.

i. <u>Countermarch</u>. Execute two forward twirls and face right about, marking time.

(1) Point the baton skyward and perpendicular to the deck, ferrule up, hand in front of face, left hand on hip. This is the preliminary position (fig 5-14A).

(2) Lower the baton from the preliminary position to a position with the ball waist-high, keeping the baton perpendicular and the ferrule skyward (fig 5-14B). This movement is executed on the weak beat or the right foot and indicates the command MARCH. The front rank of the unit counts 5 paces (commencing the count on the left foot following the command signal) and executes two consecutive right flank movements on the fifth and sixth counts. On the signal of execution, the drum major steps forward on the left foot, marching through the center of the unit. This signal is executed while facing the unit.

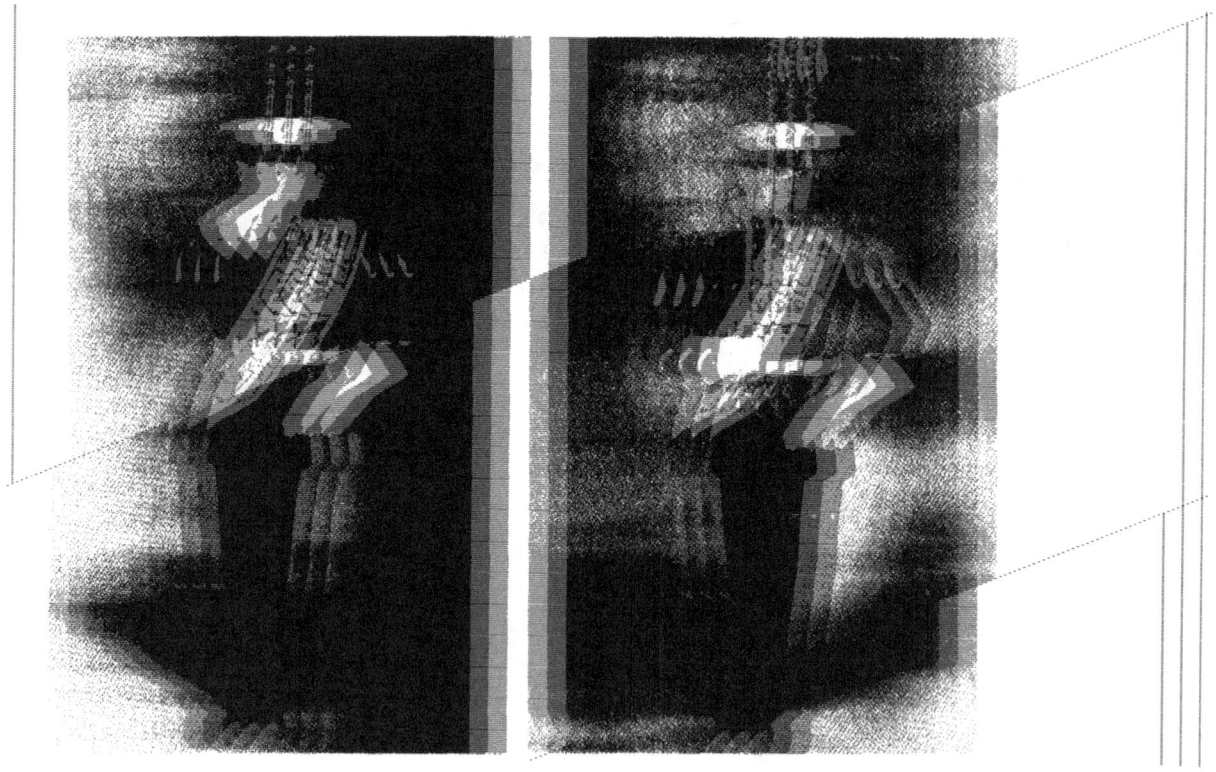

A.   B.

Fig 5-14. Countermarch.

j. Half-step. Hold the baton in both hands, shoulder high and horizontal (same as Halt, count two (fig 5-13B). This signal is executed while facing the unit.

k. Forward March from Mark-Time or Half-Step. This signal consists of two positions of one count each. In preliminary or alerting position, the baton is held horizontally by both hands, forehead-high, arms extended forward.

    (1) On count "one" (executed on the weak beat or right foot), the baton is dropped smartly to a waist-high horizontal position, arms remaining extended (fig 5-15).

    (2) On count "two" (executed on the strong beat or left foot), the baton is brought smartly to a shoulder-high position, close to the body, arms bent, baton horizontal (same as Halt, count two fig 5-13B). The unit and the drum major step off on the next left foot. This signal is executed while facing the unit.

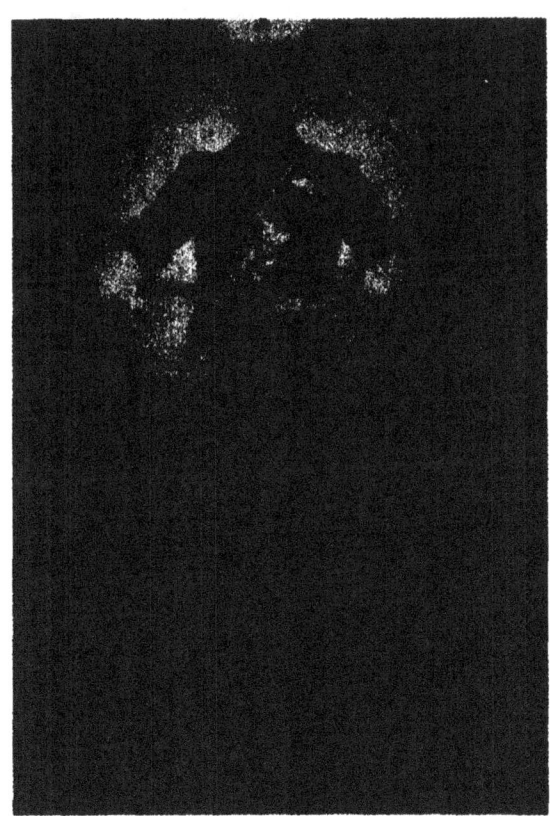

Fig 5-15. Forward March From Mark-Time or Half-Step.

1. <u>Right turn</u>. This signal consists of two positions of one count each. To assume the preliminary position, execute two forward twirls; the baton comes to rest at a position horizontal at shoulder height, ferrule pointed to the right, ball slightly to the right of the face. left hand remains on hip (fig 5-16A).

    (1) on count "one" (executed on the strong beat, or left foot), the baton is moved on a horizontal plane, approximately 12 inches to the left, ferrule continuing to point to the right.

    (2) On count "two" (executed on the weak beat, or right foot), move the baton sharply to the right, ball passing the face and stopping approximately 12 inches to the right of the face. The baton remains horizontal (fig 5-16B).

A.   B.

Fig 5-16. Right turn.

m. <u>Left turn</u>. This signal consists of two positions of one count each. To assume the preliminary position, execute two forward twirls; bring the baton to rest at a position horizontal and shoulder-high; ferrule pointing to the left, ball in front of face (fig 5-17A). Left hand remains on the hip.

   (1) On count "one" (executed on the weak beat or right foot), the baton is moved on a horizontal plane to a position approximately 12 inches to the right. The ferrule continues to point to the left (fig 5-17B)0

   (2) On count "two" (executed on the strong beat or left foot), move the baton sharply to the left, ball returning to a position in front of the face. The baton remains horizontal (fig 5-17A).

A.   B.

Fig 5-17. Left turn

n.   <u>Rolloff</u>. The baton signal for the rolloff is the same as <u>Prepare</u> <u>to Play</u> (fig 5-8). The rolloff is then performed by the percussion section on the first accented beat following the completion of the street beat being played0 On the first beat of the rolloff, the drum major executes the downbeat and returns to the Carry Baton position (fig 5-3). On the 3rd and 4th measures of the rolloff, the drum major executes two forward twirls and returns to the position of <u>Prepare to Play</u>. On the first accented beat following the rolloff, the drum major again executes the downbeat and continues with the baton beat pattern.

o.   <u>Soundoff</u>. The baton signal for soundoff is executed as follows:

(1)   The drum major faces the drum and bugle corps and verbally com-mands. SOUNDOFF, executes <u>Prepare to Play</u>, and signals the down-beat, at which time the drum and bugle corps commences to play the <u>Soundoff</u>.

(2)   <u>Cadence-baton</u> is then executed by the drum major for four counts (two measures). On the fifth count, the drum major executes <u>Port Baton</u> and faces about; on the seventh count, he executes <u>Prepare to Play</u>; and, on the next accented beat, he signals the <u>Downbeat</u>. On the first accented beat of the march, the drum major and the drum and bugle corps step off playing0

(3)   When the drum and bugle corps has halted in its original posi-tion after having trooped the line, the drum major, facing the drum and bugle corps, executes the baton signal <u>Cutoff</u>. After the completion of <u>Soundoff</u>, the drum major executes about face and faces the front.

p.   <u>Soundoff (in Place)</u>. The baton signal for <u>Soundoff in Place</u> is ex-ecuted as described above, except:

(1)   The drum major remains facing the drum and bugle corps during the entire rendition of the <u>Soundoff</u> and the subsequent march.

(2)   The drum major performs <u>Cadence Baton</u> through one strain of the march, executes the baton signal <u>Cutoff</u>, and on the next accented beat causes the drum and bugle corps to play the <u>Soundoff</u> again.

q.   <u>Correct Alinement</u>. The drum major places himself in front of and facing the right file while the unit is at the halt in marching formation. The baton is held in the same position as the preliminary position for <u>Countermarch</u> (fig .5-14A). The file then dresses on the drum majors baton. When the first file is dressed properly, the drum major faces to the right, takes 2 paces, faces to the left, and repeats the alinement on the second file, then the third, and so on. This movement is executed while facing the unit.